WATER CYCLES:
Change That Matters

Written by: Jay Friday

Published under the pseudonym Jay Friday

Cover design by Vance Godfrey.

ISBN: 979-8-9945575-0-1

Self-published.
Printed in the United States of America.

First edition, March 2025

TABLE OF POETIC CONENT

FOREWORD

Water comes in many forms;
Just like love,
Just like trauma,
Just like people,
Just like growth.

Different trials *could* evaporate our joy.
Situations we go through *could* turn our hearts into ice.
Unexpected events *could* make it hard to go with the flow.

The circumstances that shape us,
Don't always determine the state of our being.
Even if what matters doesn't change,
The changes we go through,
always matter.

EVERY TEARDROP IS A DOWNPOUR

DROPS: THE DESCENT

I cry when it rains.
I remember losing you like it was this morning.
No night of rest has occurred since you were laid to yours.
I often wonder if you'd be proud of me.

I cry when it rains.
The sky always seems to open up when I refuse to.
Depression has been getting what I can never give others, the best of me.
People say time heals all wounds, but I beg to differ.

I cry when it rains.
I have grown into this anger that never really suited me.
It's always on my worst days that I remember red is not one of my favorite colors.
That could be the reason that malice always transitions to melancholy.

I cry when it rains.
Things always slip through my fingers.
I can't hold on to anything that I deem important anymore.
Water comes back in new forms, just like my anxiety.
It's been this same cycle since December 28th, 2008.
I can't do anything these days, but *cry*.

THE BATTLE

You've got your claws in me again.
Tried to run from you and stumbled off the deep end.
You crept up,
I got swept up,
Now I'm drowning in my emotions.
Waves of sadness crashing over me,
Survival seems like just a notion.
I barely made it out of the barrel.
Drifting further from my sanity,
This *depression* is feral.
Sunk its teeth into my heart,
Now I'm bleeding blue.
Debating whether or not I want to save myself,
'Cause every piece of me I lose,
Is another lost fight against my mental health.
My absence erases the impact I've had on someone else's life.
Imagine looking in the mirror and seeing a stranger.
Constantly alerting my own sense of fight or flight.
How do you run away when you are the real danger?

INFATUATION'S DAUGHTER

Being *infatuated* is kinda like eating junk food.
Whenever the urge strikes,
I want to consume and inhale you more than air.
Later, when I'm alone,
I regret it.
Lana sang of Diet Mountain Dew, but alcohol is a better description of my *addiction* to you.
"You're no good for me, but baby, I want you, I want you."
Being drunk with denial,
Leaves me feeling like I need to visit LA: Lovers Anonymous.
I'm sick.
I have a problem.
It's too easy for me to fall head over heels for people I know will never catch me.
Completely asinine how much I love arsenic filled kisses.
I'm something of a masochistic sadist.
The way I break my own heart can't possibly be described by any other means.
If only I could learn to love myself that quickly.
Maybe I wouldn't have gotten this damaged in the first place.
However,
That's where I'd be if this was a broken heart race.
In 24 years, I've had my heart broken numerous times.
I can't say my father was the first man to ever break my heart because he's done just the opposite.
Never asked questions,
Just found a way to pick up my jagged edges and piece them back together.

That might explain why his hands are so rough.
Whereas my mom's hands are delicate.
She's found ways to mop over the tracks of my tears.
Made a goon of my grandmother and sent her to handle her light work.
She may have been raised single-handedly,
But it's a team effort when they raze me.
I may have inherited their vertigo since looking for my own self-confidence has always made me dizzy.
The first and second of five women to break my heart.
They learned heartache at young ages.
Craved attention because no daddy ever gave it to them.
No crown with princess written on it,
Only thorns from roses they could never afford and Cinderella as nicknames.
Left alone to pick up the broken pieces of their mothers after drunken bouts of their fathers.
Used to other men using their work boots to turn them into welcome mats for disappointment.
Learned to flinch from raised hands.
Hands always in the air grasping for a god to restore their sanity,
For somebody to hear their pleas.
Maybe that's why their backs always seem to bend that way.
It's as if they're hiding from gravity on knees filled with arthritis from praying too much.
3 generations of heart broken women before me so maybe it was always in my blood.

DISASTEROLOGY

Trace your fingers along my jagged edges.
Let me cut you into a million pieces,
Watch your blood intertwine with my words.
Shatter me.
I promise to break easily.
We are a mosaic of all that is lost and broken.
Your mind for loving me,
My heart for trusting you.
Is this all that we were meant to be?
A brilliant masterpiece of the ugly things we couldn't hide.
My insecurities, imperfections and idiosyncrasies drove you away.
You, lacking patience, persistence and perseverance, refused to stay.
To any new lover,
I extend this invitation:
Bare the scars of your past with mine.
Allow me to tell you what I've been through,
So you can tear me to shreds from the inside.

ERUPT

When I die
I want to be cremated
I want my corpse to be the same as my living entity always was
Engulfed in and consumed by flames
Utterly decimated by heat too hot to handle
I am a woman,
Always burning
Burning with lust
Burning with anger
Burning brilliantly in my own hatred
My insides
Are all smoke and ash
Wisps of black smoke
Fill my chest cavity
Where a heart
Charred 5 too many times used to reside
Toxic fumes run through my veins
Waiting for just the right spark to spontaneously combust
My tongue
Has a habit of scorching things
It will brand your skin in my desire
Then turn and brand your mind with my words of either love, dismissal, or a potent combination of both
I have come to the realization
That I am more than constantly on fire, burning
I am volcanic
I settle, for long periods of time

Yet, when shaken to my core,
I erupt
I consume
I destroy
Nothing and no one in my vicinity is safe
When you hear the sound of sirens,
It is best to take your leave while you still have a chance.
There is no escaping my landslide of lava like emotions
They flow too quickly.

Vapors Are Clouds Too

DROPS: SATURATION

I wonder why it rains.
I'm not sure which is louder between the thunderstorm,
And the thundering disappointment in my mother's voice.
The image of her princess washed away a while ago.
All that's left is this stranger drenched in sin.

I wonder why it rains.
Is it the culmination of thoughts and dreams deferred accumulating in cumulus clouds?
I'm walking this tightrope,
Trying to balance between my aspirations and sanity.
The more you choose one, it seems that the other slips away.

I wonder why it rains.
Maybe it's better that I appear more nimbus than numb.
It's a bit of a gray area.
Being blue is not the only common denominator between me and the sky.
We both only get relief after pouring everything out of ourselves.

I wonder why it rains.
Mama always told me to get my head out of the clouds.
She never told me how to get the clouds out of my head though.
I get strung up like stratus,
Suspended somewhere between time and the gravity of my mistakes.

I wonder why it rains.
Sometimes,
I feel that lightning and I have a special relationship.
It always illuminates everything in my darkest moments.
The truth is something I've been running from.
I wonder why...

A Girl That I Once Knew

You remind me of a girl that I once knew
She had the stars embedded in her eyes
Forever smiling
In love with who she was.
Flamboyant as could be
Artistic
A whirlwind of song lyrics and dance
Confident to those that saw her even though she struggled with self esteem
Benevolent, gentle soul she was.
It's a shame she passed away...

Died of too many heartbreaks.
The pain got too real for her.
Each star turned black hole until the light was consumed
She smiled less, cried more.
Learned to fall in love with hating herself
Her flamboyancy left by the wayside with each scripture
The art she used to love tied a noose around her neck
It became harder to choke out the lyrics.
Dancing seems so unusual on puppet strings
Sank deeper into the depths of herself than the Titanic ever could
Became jagged around the edges
All of her surfaces picked up her former bad habits and are out for blood.

They wonder why she's so angry these days.
Why is she so sad?
Maybe she would still know how to fill voids and be whole
Had her identity not been torn in half.

The Apology

Losing touch with you has been painful.
I couldn't say whether or not I still loved you,
I mean, I tried to.
Things you've put me through made me think you're the devil.
You hurt my family.
Pushed me away from my friends.
Made decisions that left both physical and mental scars on me.
Turned me into nothing more than a disappointment.
For a long time,
I wondered how you could be so cruel?
Where was your humanity?
I prayed to escape you.
I prayed that you would die so that your grip on me was gone.
It took a while for me to realize this,
But I should apologize.
I never showed you the love that you needed.
It was hard when other people viewed you as they did.
You were so loud that some labeled you obnoxious.
You were too smart so people stayed away from you because they felt you'd make them feel inferior.
You were too thin to be slim thick,
Then you were too fat.
You walked in a funny way.
Your style was too eccentric to be considered normal.
Your mental illnesses and all the medication made you crazy.
How could I be satisfied with you when you were always less than my definition of perfect?

You battled cancer and I still never viewed you as strong even though others did.
I guess the fault wasn't in the stars but in my mind.
I grew sick of hearing your name.
Sick of seeing your face.
Tired of people asking about you...
I should've acknowledged your battles,
Noticed the strength it took for you to carry on when you could barely pick yourself up out of bed most days.
I need to get the venom out of my system.
Until I can address you properly,
No apology will be good enough.
Jeannine Brenette Friday.
I am sorry I loved other people so easily when I couldn't love you.
I made you feel subhuman for what you were not and could never be.
However,
I won't just try to love and respect you,
I will.
I promise Jeannine that I will love you.
It's finally time that I learn to love myself...

STRUT

Shoulders back,
Back arched,
Head high,
One foot in front of the other,
Now move.
Stay beautiful, strut with confidence.
Don't let them see you trip.
They want to see you fail,
Fall over your insecurities.
That pigeon toed,
Bow-legged,
Knock-kneed saunter around your thighs,
They think you're switching.
You're just trying to stay upright.
I hope no officer ever asks you to walk a straight line.
Hips don't lie,
But mine testify.
They tell of the long line of baby-birthing, independent women.
You can stare,
But you can't dream of touching them.
I am out of your league and once I move past you,
You are out of time.
My walk is sublime
Jelly may jiggle but the booty quakes
My thighs are equivalent to tectonic plates
I rip through the fabric of your expectations.
Earth can't handle how fabulous I am when I'm feeling my-

self.
Now if only I felt this way most days.
I try to walk faster than my insecurities.
I try not to let them get the best of me,
But the way my hands tremble when walking past a group of strangers tell me that my mind affects the rest of me.
I will not crumble beneath the pressure,
But this crystallization hurts.
I wonder if my heels click louder than the voices that tell me to shrink back.
I guess there's only one way to find out.
Shoulders back,
Back arched,
Head high,
One foot in front of the other,
Breathe...
Now move.

WHO I BE

The strangest encounter happened today
I entered a realm within myself
So deep within my subconscious that I became unrecogniz-
able
There was a woman there
She asked me who I was
"Who am I? Who are you?"
She replied "Child. I know who I am but I fear you can't
answer your own question. So, I'll ask differently. Who might
you be?"
Now, this plagues me
They see religious girl brought up in upstanding family full
of love
I see repression
Look in the mirror and see hatred
People wonder why when you're somewhat aesthetically
pleasing
Others see living out loud queer black jawn
Really, is that true?
Identity still a question mark to both me and you
I'm called she and it makes me cringe at times
Yet "they" is still elusive and not acknowledged by enough
people
Who might I be?...
I be all and none
A pangaea of identities
I be repression
But loud and care free some days

I be hatred
Willing to love in the deepest ways
I be my biggest supporter
And somehow the worst enemy I'll ever face
I be destruction and devastation
Transitioning into tranquility and restoration
Still going through this maze of emotions
I be lost in my own darkness
Yet found by the light within myself
I be forever learning
Just to cope with my mental health
I be colder than ice cold
But molten lava at the core
I be the rhythm that keeps you moving
And the melody that soars
I be the least likely hero
The one you needed but never knew
I be bending myself until I break
Yet be my own glue
I be the catalyst
This reaction starts when I say go
Yet I also be the blocker so it stops when I say so.
I be a reflection of the universe
The stars reside within me
I be full of love, shining brilliantly with positive energy
Now that I know who I am,
I'll hold onto it securely.

JUST AROUND THE RIVERBEND

DROPS: ASCENSION

I dance when it rains
Fully engaged in my own joy like a child
The raindrops cascade through my curls
The raindrops caress my curves

I dance when it rains
Washing away my insecurities
Feeling the pelting rain on my skin
Knowing that the dawn of something beautiful is on the horizon

I dance when it rains
I cleanse myself of you
Raindrops wash away the tracks that your hands followed
They lift the feel of you from my lips

I dance when it rains
Picking up speed
Moving faster than my anxieties
I spin in circles around my own disillusions
Jumping in puddles instead of to conclusions

I dance when it rains
My tears flow
Creating my own rainbow of emotions
Colors exploding just like drops when they hit the ground

I dance when it rains
Fully engaged in my own joy like a child

I dance when it rains
Washing the memories from my lips
I dance when it rains
Speaking freedom into existence
I dance when it rains
I dance when
I dance

REINTRODUCTION

Allow me to reintroduce myself.
My name is Jay Friday.
J A Y F R I D A Y
Joy Always Yields Fruitage Reflected In Divinity And Youth.
My birth name means "God's precious gift",
Since I've graced this earth,
That's what I have been.
The importance of self love is the only thing I'm stressing.
Let me reiterate.
I am both blessed and blessing.
Y'all heard me when I told y'all Who I Be.
It took a while for me to get in touch with myself,
But now my mindset and my reality are the same,
Free.
I am by no means perfect.
Friday doesn't always define the weekend,
Yet,
I know I'm worth it.
I've carried my stake,
Assured that I've earned every success I come across.
Shrinking,
Is something my fro does,
Not my personality.
This evolution is an ongoing process.
Even when reaching your destination in the past seemed unlikely.
Progress is progress,
Don't take any step made in the right direction lightly.

ISLANDS (ERUPT CONT'D.)

The devastation and chaos,
Are not all that comes from this.
I give birth to islands.
Each one a new lesson learned.
The land gains fertility.
Just like nature,
I bounce back as a healthier version of myself.
The things I have uprooted,
Those bridges I've burnt,
Have all been for the betterment of my being.
I settle once again.
Becoming just a little more comfortable with who I am.
So when I die,
I want to be cremated.
Plant my ashes with the soil and roots of a tree.
Even in death,
My growth will not be forgotten.

GROWTH

A familiar encounter happened today.
I entered a realm so deep within my subconscious,
That I faded away into the background.
There was a woman there,
In the mirror.
She looked me directly in the eye and said:

"The embodiment of light is what you've become.
Pulled yourself from your own darkness.
The insecurities you once had look at you and cower in fear
They don't recognize you.
A change,
Growth,
Has taken place within.
You've reached out to become the better version of yourself,
Like that sunflower that stretches towards the sky.
Nothing can stand in your way except that person you see before you,
And you have chosen to never let them bring you down again.
The voices inside of you,
Now shout affirmations of your self love and beauty.
You are worthy of every opportunity that comes your way.
Cosmic energy surrounds you.
Be sure of your steps.
This is the era where you conquer all that you come across.
Reclaimed your identity
You are nothing short of remarkable

Phenomenal woman,
Maya would be proud of you too.
So keep your head held high
The sky is not a limit but a resting place for you.
Never allow the winds of negativity to extinguish your internal flame
Burn brilliantly with determination.
Remember that your transformation may not have been easy,
But it is a beautiful one.
From this day forward,
You are no longer living in the shadows,
But you are a daughter of the Sun.
Do not shrink back or be afraid of what you are capable of.
Know that you are everything you've ever needed to be,
The culmination of hard work, and self-love."

FLUIDITY

I wish I could become water
Make myself harder than what hurt me
Able to take blows and reemerge as if nothing ever happened
Displaying fluid emotions but never uncontrolled
Battered hearts beat differently when they turn to ice

I'm trying to become water
Realizing that stagnation breeds unwanted things
I move.
I flow freely.
Overcoming obstacles and rushing past anything in my way

I'm learning to become water
Defy my dreams and the greater the pressure I exert to realize them
Try to get me heated and I will rise above the drama
Undermine my determination and my success will turn into a torrential downpour
You cannot grasp or hold back what I am becoming

I've become just like water,
Metamorphic and powerful.

ACKNOWLEDGEMENTS

I want to acknowledge some very special individuals that helped make this possible. Thank you to my immediate family for always supporting me, and helping me through the metamorphosis that needed to take place. Thank you Ms. Gina Henry, my middle school English teacher. Without your love, guidance, and encouragement, I would not be the poet that I am today. Thank you to my grandfather, Mr. George Gray, for being my biggest supporter and one of my favorite people. The wisdom and knowledge you've imparted to me over the years have given me a glimpse of another world. I love all of you dearly.

There are so many other people, places, and experiences that helped shape the version of me that I am now. I was poured into, and encouraged beyond measure. The love that I was privileged enough to take in, helped push out the toxicity that I felt flowing through me. I shared my journey in hopes that anyone that feels frozen in time, drowned in depression, or overwhelmed with overcast skies, may have the strength to change. Whether those changes are internal or external, they are necessary. Keep flowing.

www.ingramcontent.com/pod-product-compliance
Lightning Source LLC
LaVergne TN
LVHW020629110826
845149LV00004B/1117

* 9 7 9 8 9 9 4 5 5 7 5 0 1 *